Paper Head Last Lyrics

Other books by Andrew Levy

between poems
Values Chauffeur You
Democracy Assemblages
Curve
Song From My Family
Continuous Discontinuous—Curve 2
Elephant Surveillance To Thought

Paper Head Last Lyrics

Andrew Levy

ROOF BOOKS
NEW YORK

for
D.R. Miller

ISBN: 0-937804-83-5
Library of Congress Catalog Card No.: 00-101561

Grateful acknowledgments to the editors of the following publications in which some of this work previously appeared: *Aufgabe, Barrow Street, Big Allis, Boomerang!, Conjunctions, Kenning, Open Letter*, and to the editors of *Telling It Slant: Avant Garde Poetics of the 1990s*, forthcoming from University of Alabama Press. The title, "An Indispensable Coefficient of Esthetic Order," is taken from John Dewey's "The Organization of Energies" in *Art As Experience*.

Cover art (c) 2000 Sally Etta Sheinfeld
Author photograph (c) 2000 Sally Etta Sheinfeld

Roof Books are distributed by
Small Press Distribution
1341 Seventh Avenue, Berkeley, CA. 94710-1403.
Phone orders: 800-869-7553
spdbooks.org

State of the Arts
NYSCA

This book was made possible, in part,
by a grant from the New York State Council on the Arts.

ROOF BOOKS
are published by
The Segue Foundation
303 East 8th Street
New York, NY 10009
segue.org

Contents

Paper Head Last Lyrics

Show me the meaning of the Word
Cause I've heard so much about it
It's said you can't live without it
Chrissie Hynde

They are said to be in the book,
        but there is no book.

One might paint the entire world, and
        in any manner one wished.
        It is almost as if one might write
        the entire world too.
What do you want, strange man?

        from where all arts and all stories came

        between grey lines on a gray page

        Viva las revoluciones!

        Now the zone that files you somewhere
        every diet pill you took

        They are sad to be
                but there is
One might point to and tire of
        The man was whisked away
        almost as if retreating from

        here all art and all memory

        every direct take you took
                spine scrunched in mattress

Money on the sacred wheel of fortune.

        tyranny as being the man of pen

There are questions from the radar.

to convey, translate, transfer
colonize the writer's fairness

On behalf of the search committee
good fortune in your career

to use the gun to kill the Imperialism

filtered somewhere and dictated towards

(which is a human being)

A young man's five minute walk

A gentle piece of reaching.
The gentle takes their reasons.

a gentle piece of machinery

A sense of entitlement

if you always check the red
and white service

Anytime. Anywhere.

HERE

tenth pouch of hell

A friend in the market is better than

your mind is filled by new ideas
Human selfishness and self-centeredness

light stuff like eggs and potato
menu covered with liver and tongue

please join us to . . .
against that tyranny as being the man

Wishes really do come true

innumerable phenomena enter

There are questions from the reader
filled in with new ideas

popcorn Levinas

was devoted to his work

tenth punch of the bell

One two three four five six rolls of
your madness momentarily slipped away

A friend in the target is better
    than chalk

your mind is somewhere else

    minds are mingling and tingling

Swollen twice its
    normal
    to be in the book

    Last Songs

    Adonai Eloheinu
    in English
    in real estate

There is also a lawnmower

retired with dignity, actually
beside the pickup truck

your mind is chilled

More than a custodian having a lucid moment
                you held up
            the stagecoach in the rain

        to be an honest narrator by refraining

            Dress for the tableau in pure and delicate

No, I think I can get a job.
            transform passersby into shadows

            no bad side effects

        following my return from Mexico

        like any genetically altered human

In fact, there is no window either,
                but only shape.

        a gentle piece of memory

                    the
                    if
                    the

            both worked themselves to death at an early

        Do you lick the paper?
        Did you once upon a time lick?

        Now is wandering
                man's wife
            a poet and colleague of mine

What day is the day of return?

the very reality of the society's one-sided judge-
mental approach

A beggar is considered a stigma
on the face

to be born helpless or was later
robbed of his equal

the loyal group turned against the master
dictated towards decisions

New ways to improve the techniques of writing

a small window not far from the restrooms

raw populism (like raw onion)
a refuse in adversity

Now I see what kind of danger you give up

"Well," she said after exhaling, "something else."

When the moon is in the seventh house
and Jupiter aligned with Mars

This is the dawning of the age of Aquarius
On the laundromat radio

"But tonight is different," she pushed on.

Who socked Madonna?

the three-dimensional arrangement
of emotion in language

A traffic island

I know when you are not being honest with

nice typo

Black and orange on a buff background.

listening to St. John's wort
"we will not be defined by our temperature"

camera-ready?

No, I think I can transform passersby into
psychological processes

Once man's aspirations bed money

disappear completely
perish time

peace will guide the planets

No one has been able to prove it.

No one has
been able
to prove it.

A little piece of machinery

Raw populace like rare bunion or rough pumice?

In moving slow he has no peer.

he says he's a space alien
alright, that's enough, no more
kisses.

Henry Kissinger is one evil
son of a bitch.

No one can understand what I'm talking about.

"slime nose & green lip"

Henry Kissinger is an evil

The handle of a carpet sweeper

purple rain
bovine spongeaform disease
        cows eating sheep

He's completely in control.

the presence of others
        sober false dung pundits
I seem to remember

the more ground we gain, the more
                ingrown we become

Overall, response is "perverse"

It is a work wild with astonishing craft
        that screams through the early

Audrey says, a man, engulfed by the flames,
        stands still as if accepting
        his own demise.

crickets quietly sing them to sleep

I guess civil disobedience is contagious

You shock my senses
my sense of metabolism

So, the boys made a pact . . .

The horrible thought of being captured
        by the Russians

Everything is under control now.

Abraham is the connection to your old
world roots.

fuck you

Amonth the other pieces, the one

Love to swallow the line and your hand.

She loved ideas more than bodies

Translation: You can go through or over
pretty much anything.

pretty, pretty . . .

curves and curves

Recruited men, not rhinoceros, not tiger.
total consciousness of the limits of words

Used because of its purity.

moon close to man in the next line, literally

Purple sky

The society of the elders has resulted
                In some candid conversations
That have revealed a few new facts.

rather than as an unfinished fragment

I'm made out of clay

"norming" intellectual activity in the organic whole

did not know you to be the one to
                suffer Gandhi . . . dreamt that.

Don Quixote!

I'm made out of glue

Yoy not joy

I don't *feel* hungry.

a kind of post-contentment that intervenes
                in the present

the awakening may come about

A refuge in diversity

peace will guide the carpet sweeper

every tree has set upon its head a tray

I love to swallow you

facilitated by two consultants with extensive familiarity

Slime notes & green lips

language as repertoire, adventures in
                    numbed reading

The different fell time bought to place work here, hmn.

the trees the bees the knees all scuffed and scurvy

An apprenticeship with Allen Ginsberg

and when it's dry and ready, my dreidel
also known as Dracula . . .

in the laundromat clothes are mingling

My spine is tingling

almost as if retreating from
the machinery
the pen

the keys on this fingerpad in this instance

this omniscience on screen

I made it out of clay

we journeyed from archetype to archetype,
                laying the path

storms that are impossible

                devil in evening dress
        chaperon of decay

An apparently normal woman may have some
                genetically male tissues
from what originated as her twin brother,
                or vice versa.

        a reawakening of protoplasm

A large part of writing, he'd heard it said
        has to do with forgetting . . .

        don't indulge other swoons
                don't permit your vote to be high and
                                shrill
        don't publicly knot every time you invest

Yvonne said, I kissed the girl opening the rope
                even though I had a great date who gives
                                blow jobs.

        drinking electric water

everyone around us knows how to read and write

I'm an ordinary woman

it shrunk up on me

Did you lick the pap?
Did you nurse?

to be reminded of his inheritage
called the legs

one has to use this ladder

If I wanted to turn somebody
on to de Sade, I'd say *Justine*

image of a cannon being fired at the clouds

I think what Claudius is doing here . . .

Are people restless?

the background radiation of parody
"nobody fucks with Jesus"

Six Flags Egypt

star-crust lovers
their Egypticism

crisp
pretty much as I wrote it

She thinks she has a child
And she doesn't

it didn't belong (in the world)

You've gone back to who you always were

you like them

Have faith in this present piece

he ate his heart
he was never mistaken for someone else

what will you do once you arrive

Large and uncut looking for AM action

You are going to die

evaporated parts of himself
he let go to the sky

you like them a lot

lack of sugar, butter
impedes either yellow or blue

determines green
(implying that we are near the shoreline)

sharing a sexual secret

Somebody is living on this beach
always being washed away

An emerging genre of cheerfully
subversive poetry

Oh, Oh bay-bee . . .

the abysmal stupidity of insects

his chameleon thing inside

as it rises to the surface all the nerves go bloomy

Those who choose the path of license are completely deaf
                    And hear nothing.

He paid a very high price for everything. So did she.

        an intelligentsia separate from itself
                Would think 'postmodernism' is that

    Given the last 'sentenced

        A good poem, he said, has no intention
                of disavowing

In this country I have seen three different things:

                        An excruciating capacity for endurance
            An identification of faith with patience
                An investment of power in the exploitation
                        of this accursed patience.

        Also, a heyday for semi-literacy "funded"
                the ruling elite

    perish time

somebody is living on this rage

self-critical try frying pork chops

"self-critical poetry" a coinage of
        self-critical writers? of poems?

rushes to be washed away

since you bid this night thing goodbye

Have faith in this present piece of paper

he ate his hat

nobody could ever mistake him for someone else

'You sell my soul for a handful of dust'

    two old women on folding garden chairs
            On the same stoop
    pointing index fingers at each other . . .
    "You're crazy!" "Who's crazy?!"
            "You're crazy!"

the Excedrin coursing through my veins

I spelt with Mr. Spicer when I was 5
    I think I know him better than you

These are not the most outstanding books
        written by anyone

2 sexes, 3 standards
solid and handsomely mounted

        these were the moments that
        appeared to him in the form of attention
            he'd come to feel at home in.

I always walk around with
a dish in my mouth

exercise: cup up several different comic
strips and rearrange—

I would rather be run over by a truck

the body is the
soul perceived
thru the 5 senses
I wrote that in the dark on a
violet colored paper

the ire between the sentimental
and the metaphysical
or
nothing is in the room

Hand over hand up the
length of the bat

expression of a principle
inside the visible world

pure of sin and blemish

Sandbox

more fiddling
a moment perpetuated forever

pages falling out of spine of book
hope abandoned

spice of book

the world map in a small holographic eclipse, green
pavement of gold bullion

Prison stories

Abject adulation is their common goal.

a leap into delinquency
Nietzsche's scattered waste

Zen has no tunnel. Zeno, on the other
Alright now, you take care, ya hear—Okey dokey . . .

Thursday the 146th, end of an assassin

Dear /system sunshine,
have felt craushed (?)

You could argue with what it's saying

the evanescence and insubstantiality of cold
shudders in the belly

An unleveling of thought in the ether of a new space?

a shooting star succeeding through sheer perversity
as though innumerable transparent tissues hovered
over the same strip of film

A key unlocks my entire life
     brittle ice in beautiful limbs

postmodernism would never be mistaken for the bank
     And watch, the hands of my partner

the sentence undulates

And we are always here

and the trees, the splendid fuel, the flowers seem, free relations,
          deadly fish, the proverb, flourishes, the dust in the, immediate
or yesterday, the phone, horizons are, the curves, the unwanted,
               places of night, my friend's, is soft

Continual thought grain was to eat

obligations and cautions

Wherever fourth base is
I want her to go there
(4th base is really 1st base)

the dagger of an immutable income

'Like a gondolier's paddle, this lass stirred up much
from the bottom of my stagnant canals.'

little bits of slime
"from the bottom of my stagnant canals"?

the danger of an immutable tenure
has no turmoil

Man. What a shock
to the *cogito*

like to shoot his jam

breaks its spine

plunged last Monday, levitating
by Friday

Ran out of nuclear rods

"The Buddha has smiled."

not to be found in any calendar

a sufficient advertisement to
hard-boiled barking accents of business

a New Englander of the deepest dye

Why should I be impatient
I have prepared my defense

Dogs barking somewhere in the neighborhood

ears ringing late at night
don't know why

penmanship gone totally to hell
spine too

stomach speaking, penis
stiffening as he read *Wittengenstein's
Mistress*

A Midwesterner in love with
transformation

kindergarten needs no further
metaplasm

everything is still all lilac
covered with leaves
I was able to verify that I had ever even

with fluffy cottonwood seeds

underlining sentences in books that had not
been assigned

and from this day did become the daughter
of what I did pay attention to

after coffee, his large too
much mouth

from here it's possible to see
what he is doing

there's baloney in my slacks . . .

I take back everything I said.

Summer's bathtub-full of brussels sprout

shouting prophecies and curses

'globalization' will continue to provide
child labor
This is the rebel's reward

the caffeine coursing through my brain

Think on the devil

We'll keep you posted
to hold up the trembling structure

sub-me, sub-keep in the gooey ball-bearing

Metal, metal
rabid ears
power and sex among apes

the more familiar spongy proteinaceous material

synthesizing sugar from sunlight
thoughts powered by the undulating motions
of their flagella

Beethoven, the Bose advertisement

An 'unwieldy idea'

I'll never say no to a glass of wine
was only 5' 4"
and you are not in my arms

computers and videos convey
the message that
biodiversity

even the money looks good

or yesterday, the phone, horizons are, the curves, the unwanted,
places of night, my friend's, is soft

Continual thought rain was to seat
obbligatos and cautions

the tips of bamboo leaves eludes me

To releaf all inhibitions . . .
distant trip swells with memories
Salt and pepper bear upon its head
a slender white hand
the form of a bed
don't know when to return, when to go home

Leisurely, slowly, with hesitation
with promises of Persia

someone calling into the empty air

Literary publishers tied naked to a huge oak
in Persia

A mirror flying across the sky
shattered his point-of-sale

Make a new life

paper head last lyrics

It's smaller than you can see

the coldness without which one could not live
An abracadabra, open sesame

somebody is living on this beach
                    always being washed away

the reading of adipose or other swoons

don't supplement the supernumerary

My Tasmanian developer

the very character of it which calls our attention to it
let it come back

to drive a bayonet into a Buddhist priest's guts

with choir, blame, damages
their liar
"testing their intelligence"

Hey, watch-u wanna doo
Watch-u wanna doo
bay-bay . . .
bay-b—a—y

His father said he'd have to *learn* to enjoy TV

easy skanking

Seinfeld Girlfriend.
Frasier Niles damages floor.

Male. Very discreet.
　disqualified
　far back in the trees

　"red channels"

　A fascist conspiracy
　Hollywood fights back?

I look backwards and forwards.

"Writing turns us into what we're turning into."

They're all idolaters and losers, he said.

There was nothing romantic about this.

　riot-gear in Disneyland
　　A rubber ego, not soul . . .

Falling into the trap of the demon, that would be
　A tragedy

look for the answer in the same place that you found the elephant

It is from the mind that our bodies have learned to rave

unravel the game of adoration

This idea does not cross his mind.

　Little bits of slime
unlocks my entire life
brittle ice in her beautiful

I WAS BORED

He died in battle with a king
           He was cooked on a slow fire and eaten.

degradation, or "mechanized petrification
           embellished with a sort of convulsive
                 self-importance," as described
                             by Max Weber

His tongue is long enough to clean
         his johnson, and if you get
             too close, yours.

consolation is the glue

I'll hit them with my spank-ray!

took a look at the air
arbitrary conceptions go up in smoke

I don't want to have to answer to these thirds.

Part your way from the paddle
                          meant for me
paperhead lay lysergic make a new life
                & take back everything once said

don't even think

the whole whale
5 poems (one word per line) I like

Daddy never keeps his

perhaps the only jaws in Oklahoma

my friend who's diabetic
        Gone to the river & there's a reason why
because the river's druy

I'd rather be here than any place I know

Faced with a frequently malign universe, he can never
Quite bring himself to choose between his pleasure
In the improvisatory shifts of strategic retreat and his
Impulse to love some creature palpably weaker and more
Threatened than himself.

fallibility and phobia

That's all you see all the time; this is what I want to do

There's no reason why every body shouldn't have
a novel in it, or a CD-ROM

Meet me on the corner of 6th and Avenue A
It'll be wearing a long gray hemp skirt

she made it out of play

it's genuine . . .)

give yourself away

"we go into significance and drive"
its dream said

Associations with intellectuals will rub off

on the architectures they live in

Impatient
'replicas of emotion', says Alex

(to learn) to keep good soldiers

obligations and cautions

Not hopeful or less they say.
This is very important, read it again.

holsters for mobile phones . . .

"this language is discontinuous,
get it away from me"

Is inadequate, is
barely nil

What is it you want it to be a part of?

What is it you want?

This is your honorarium, cells
        swathed in sugar molecules

chauffeur   upside down, scrutinising holds

        unstable signal come

        their perquisites
scrawled after blunt

    A sense of entitlement, tenth pouch of hell . . .

        handful of dust

    What will you do once you arrive?

Your mind is chilled, a gentle piece

        immediate periphery
            on evidence   and samples

        you tune (and rub   )

devil in evening dress . . . stagecoach in the rain

Let me see what this I can do
                corner of your mouth
                and what led to it

or was it *Mr. Tambourine Man*?

the wheel disintegrated when they tried to pack it

            Sinatra Widow Mugged
                (your mind is chalked, then shilled)

I'm willing to live wherever I am . . .
                that's all it is

I live in your brown eyes,
                the browns in Miró
            befitting emblems of adversity
                nocturnal declension of the soul

'the artifice of eternity'

curved like new moon, moon-luminous
                seventh flower, clear water

and I love you for it

            beneath the horn of the sacrum
                            (rub there)

go on a diet and go crazy

        Yellow boa

        Memory may be read ahead of its source
before the materiality of that future

        Your I: your mail folder

eat it now

"I will not succumb to the scum"

Where my house is, I'd like
to go back there

A meat umbrella
Your
the materiality of that bread

disdain swept back the meatlight

too much anagrammatic wisdom
the slug in the ear
Papercut dividend desert mist teal headache fireman proscenium to it

keep good scholars in want

Arithmetic goes crazy

'real fright' on the screen—this is very impoverished
Shoot it again
I am not the NRA

cowardly clichés, offensive

we will come to understand through
this story

playing you sometime for your amusement

didn't you?

radio boat against hate

Never been inside the bodyguard's head

filled with loose confection

Weight of hands on tabletop
these eyes resting behind closed lids
clenched lace
on on on inordinate nothing named
whelmed emblem old growth meat

wealthiest city in the world

birds singing deterrence

walking down the drain and laughing

I'm lying

(the disease I have described is a disease of boneheads)

"objects" of a verdant and luxurious exchange
these were still "   " times

how many mistakes can it contain

back problems that no one can buy

fermenting herds like the shape(lessness) . . .
rummages in it without moving it from its place
it was a splendid work that I was looking at with pleasure

A half century passed, maybe six months

even in its fragments

"Gonzales goes fishing, and fans . . ."

warmth from my monitor portends

portals poor tents

the wealth

"A snake-like beauty in the living changes of syntax"

tabloid no resemblances echo

herd of silence of money

each other's brains *eaves* of retinal "was"

Gonzales goes fishing and fans . . .

will not beat a path to your door

                    our delicate intention would make our knees

                              bones and yes of a large flesh
          to treat people like oxygen
                              implies a depository

          Something can happen from you gracefully;
                                        returning every breath

                    Maybe six months

               the body of his son on his knees

                    the look accustomed to

            the revolutionary synonym societal efficiency
                    electronic restrain ribbons explanation

          electron added as a menace to the nation

               Peninsula

          I wonder why you're not kissing me yet

                    can see

          this permission has received a natural death

          with forked tongue plus fat head
                         a small time capitalist
                    Seeking his place

          Small pieces of his life transplanted

                 appellation
         Appalachian

         'Unteachable waywordness'
         A www wealth of the nation
                     A misleading timbre to write about it

         Where is this away-from-me?

A piece of verbal confusion: the camera will occasionally false . . .

     the length of the road on his belly
                 falsify, flash back the "reason" to make it seem
         in the realm of the inexplicable

   the very thing you missed you read carelessly

                 read it again, someone is living on this
         Supernumerary

         Marshland

   elevate surveillance to thought

                 paperhead of western history
         Once I had a lurid dream
                 I saw a cleft tree
         It had a hole in it
                 Once I had a lovely dream

the sweet body that I enjoyed

assembled here

it's the sweet air that spoke her speech
   in the tolling balisiers of crepuscular riches
the half-light of forever

Their mute excrement fiercer than caterpillars!

  its own genuflection . . .

pure vegetation

limpid simulacra 'invisible' and 'instant'

Neither the seas nor the sky, the epileptic accomplice of dirty hatred
these shovelfuls of no prism divides

to take hold, to stipulate

Suit my foot for the italic Face

captivity can the ecstasy define

The man in the telegraph office in Pickleville

'the disappearance of frogs'

intellectual Shastra

but the nationalist excess keeps me from showing up

No ideas but in effects

the improvisatory shifts of strategic re-treatment an
Impulse to love impermanent

the head of the man whose head has no bone

more than just skin, a think protection
silver light in the rented room

see if I am more bone and marrow
prehistory wash of sand cushioned the entire boot

Wake and then remember

your hair on your brow, that wondrous flesh
I cannot make you happy

poetry in the little hieratic jar? Remuneration seeking heaven?

useless world

the certain expectant force of it wrapping life
in places   or times

whenever you put in what you think

can help you

formula transmigration

I don't write out of these eyes when I sing

if you want to kill this man,
        I can help you

        the way of writing is straight and crooked?

        Yielding place to pure dimension

a mouse drowned in the cream

This is where your fool dried his tears

Think of your opponent as from the grave

        what does he do? Who to?

Doubted with a sort of convulsive self-importance
                mother "testing their intelligence"
        confronted the porridge of non-hallucinatory
                delusions

        i.e., courtly love; i.e., masochism adopted by
                State armies

        To haul or not to haul, that is
                oriented and cool

Totalitarian and fascist fibers your Goddamn mother

        Infatuated again with the palms
        she takes a steam bath with her mint tea

Oriented and cool
          in thirty-seconds this breeze will begin
          in the black hole

Hard for you to get out there and appreciate anything you see

          you don't like it

Highway 41 revisited
          Corn on the cob, fried chicken

Hole In One

title of the new Nixon biography . . .

          King for a Flicker of a Second
          rejected

God Made Me Who I Didn't Want To Be For One Goddamned Second

          Also Rejected

Leaving Indiana with a Corncob Pipe and a Pouch of Chew
          New hour-long drama on NBC

          Death of a Hog Killer Over a Bag of Feed

          still under consideration

I'm looking at a big position, a big position up ahead

          My Shoes Were Full of Cow Dung
          temporarily out of the question

          Purple People Eaters

Rogue Cheddar
(1967)

thoroughly disobedient, like most devastatingly handsome
single-men of his age are

No thoughts developed by the rays of the sun

out of a pitcher, working late

The world brings the most intimate public interest

familiarity, misery
ambition, tragedy underbrush, sluice
handcuffs, fashion
Humility, blood
above the word
below the word brings more
head of the mountain in its throat

'this outrageous calcination'

Viscera you used to run out to

Space sucked wondrous that despair formed by
Names I do not know fly in my head
Sabbath so dwarfed, overripe

your sacrifice with its shade
No account

"it's something I believe in"

"I don't need the heart or scrotum"

"the cowboy hat will do"

            this is a poem on the death of
a participatory *open sesame*

admitting math and weaknesses
                all the stars of the night
the height of unemployment
                (don't put it together

their desires being despised
            excuses, only doing his job

a one-way journey in

            flicking the sand with my toes

the sweet body that he enjoyed

they will be like it themselves

        It makes no difference, it is the most that they
                can say

What is changing does not diminish—think about that

            In each word there was something he had to say

        Negative and position of the beds raised

            the author in the soft under

A vague roulette?

and the broadening self undissolving?

spook and specter

"I'd crossed the street eating the raw corrugated beef"
I prefer Balzac

Supreme dramamine

the decomposing body goes in early

friendship looks out over it

How exact you are

the darkness of solitary brightness
Laurel & Hardy
all these people, similar figures obeying
in an Utopia
without end, deceptive faith—pointless breath

Do my words also flow from him
separate him from you

Does this black that keeps me drawn to the left
prepare him to see clearly

to create peace and love the perfect way

the patience that prepares
the black that dies away, a cold brightness

A memory of light

The turd of transcendence establishes a hillside estate:
Transcendence Hill Club

Croquet is the game of choice for its ladies
All the members are ladies at
Transcendence Hill

Every one is a gentleman, and each lady wears
Ralph Lauren chaps

Inside their bodies too

Players retreat on weekends, their Secretive
Author Besieged

This pass for admittance, as presently understood
Allows them to 'communicate' to
"unpoetic" people; their prying readership
Wants to know about the latest besieged project
a long walk on the sea wall
Only opens the gap between salary tiers
Tiers they've long since
Transcended

Conference participants
echoing the slogans of a successful 5 day coalition
of attachment-tool salesmen

Look into the depth of their souls

He's all skin

An apprenticeship with appellation

down in New Orleans you do what you gotto do
try to get closer

We went through this before

Just like ice, leave in a hurry

Remember sending this one a letter

We are born a creature of air

product gone astray in self-revelation

I think it's beyond completeness
concreteness
In anyone's eyes
ceilings drift up from the public
can seedlings of disparity

How can I work with that

if you weren't of many measures
the current in an arousal, in cadence
embittered, ripe
Inflamed in unintended duration

Life poised in plaster cast
the rhythm of water above

Only enough of both to attend

to listen to debate   embrace
and emanate diagramless

Over the campfire, boner
bottom blackened

joined a self-help labor group:

The Job is Alright, but the Pay Sucks
(JAPS)

why that line keeps coming back
In my head

whelmed emblem old growth meat

The Hannah Weiner Story

We were falling in bright obstinacy

the fractured unfathomed green

fecund donations of this pattern

'This bundle of accomplishment' (Rexroth)

Walking and thinking keep people in their place

effluvium of an overfed angel, the leathery
fears of the endless year

your lips inside my ear, say

smear as lately keeper

Smooth bark

    5, 6, 7, 8, 9, 10, 11, 12, 13, 14, 15, 16, 17, 18

I am not a professional critic

  M

everything stands out in clear outline

  N

Papercut dividend desert mist teal

Smear as lately keeper

  the smooth bark I used to think, to remember

to something instruments neglect

    which he recognizes
       falling forward
    depending on some
  generosity but no resistance
    its generous resistant echo break in two

A common mind an infinite emptiness
    the trees cannot see

  you shifted and leaned over
    the line is partial, or provisional spills
    all over me

  Its mooring is almost myself

Misery discriminates poetry

one piece of twine in the mind, one strand
            not yet a rope

    Out of focus waves

        their kindness drew from me more privacy
    the now empty primordial line of reasoning

            Overshadowed incarnation of me

Shark bit into political terms truce with objects

            the man or woman in the window

    civilization of coffee and iced perfect copy

            olive oil the world

        the melting ice, the sentiments, standing naked

            your heat in a familiar corridor
                your heart and lungs

    there is little clarity or charity to any word
            You just can't take it

                Sign your soul away to autonomy?

    More political end of how things get done
            Change the protocol to distress?

                A breakdown in surveillance

    Take another person's idea and discredit?

Compassion treatment

Inheritance brings attention railing against you

Where the fuck your bread is buttered
             are is in bed, made a marriage with big guns
                         that are more specific?

Normal inherited rhythmic functions

                Where we plug it in if this continues
                            is not disconnexion

retaining your good-guy image escape-hatch

the things that drive *me*

Values that we've hacked out by ourselves
             Everybody has their needs??

ancient epiphanies . . . protruding melon . . .

                any funky tape this phone is a problem

A kind of emptiness in human contact

                shit with no peaks and valleys
basically a handheld camera about self-perception

and I probably do the same

Motherfucker where your head is buttoned

             He wanted to control his father
who consisted of nothing

the now empty primordial line of reasoning

Overshadowed incarnation of him

Shadow of cumulus on cymbalist cast by the western sun

Caramelized light of sunset

People walking what seem now to be preordained paths home

Wish you were here

Similar to the flight of birds, all set in mind

He has been noting events 42 years

Collates them in perceptible greeting and sleeps on the bed

Worn by tabulation, by appetite

Men are timid in a commonplace world

'Gill the symbols upon the page'

Killing time with a dying thing

Intruders know what is happening

There enters a bit of their substance

the prejudiced authenticity

The authenticity we call thought

take another person's idea, and discredit

Fritz Lang Fruit Slang

What does the author say?

"retardedly enjoying Agnosticism elephants aggregate kingfishers
flinging rocks euphemistically at KKK flunkies . . ."

The long erotic long them smell

There's not even room enough to be anywhere

A friend rights: forget righteous earthmothers: arm kids

And: fungus rides elephant ass kissers

Take me to TV land

I'm not here to elevate society

The *Library Journal* can kiss Marjorie Perloff's ass!

I wandered out of my parents home and slid into my right shoulder

Heston is too sophisticated to think

lead me to your forgotten, nebulous words

Please wait . . .

I want to be loved for his methodological self-confidence?

Hey! I'm talkin' to YOU, squidbrain!

The beautiful blonde could not escape her sinful past

Mr. Big Nose.
would be loved for his methodological wit

Kingdom Come, Your Elegant Cultural Historian

Hither & thither, dither and done

I think one of the reasons for this is that he was
Such an extreme conservative, that is, such an extreme partisan of his group

European countries, on the other hand, retain screenwriters
To "invent" invisible differences

He always hated Duran Duran

their need for polarization regardless of its form

What is in your mind is what is *in* your mind?

Your ankles should tell you that

It's in the mind

every cell in speech

A piano note in the ear
each year

send me your money

A love machine

Aided and abetted

Seudat Havra-ah, the meal of consolation

levy war, conclude peace
Stress will help you to remember

"You are blessed some token in my listener's field"

Thanks for the music, and the long piece of purple rubber . . .

I am your Henry Kissinger

We enjoyed the panoramic caricature of the good

*I'll show you the bees in the
    cigarette trees,
And the soda water fountain
And the lemonade springs where the
    blue bird sings
In the Big Rock Candy Mountains.*

A happy bohemian existence, see our names in lights

Greedy sentences you have to come
the lines of the hand the heaven cut in strips your tongue

Though you say nothing, you are
Made to follow the waiter inside and acquiesce

the music takes away our pain

Your hardships are immense, even more.

We're going to show you everything

they all wanted to be messengers, red ectoplasm

kings retardedly enjoying cartoons

I am your intellectual activity
        More poetic than depository

Never before has such passion (such reverb) been devoted to syllables

        such reburnishing

Mickey and Minnie take a walk
eyes blank, ears just lines

Pretext to what?

Leaving the center of the center?

back into you

the blood in our heads gliding
in the sky of the brain

A velvet station

I am your revolutionary paper tears social status

the windless calm, the noise made by those arriving

even the eternity that I am is too tight
Has not pushed on far enough ahead to have an intuitive glimpse of the eternity
that necessarily includes this book as well

[finish thought?]

but the brothers had no mercy

He drives them away with pseudonymous stories of the faceless
an intelligible weariness

Home no saline

Industrial restructuring financial instability,
And the dynamics of the postwar U.S.

that's where we should edit

Matthew Arnold British public school Latin-based grammatically-
Complete verbalizations

incomplete sentences . . . And words . . .

My income observed at a distance, paranormal semblances of it

Copy of parity as inferior entertainment forgives
Misspellings and absences

"I like to participate a foot above the floor"

and emanate diagramless
Sweet hay . . .

Sweet hay . . .

i.e., paranormal semblances of complete sentences

everything that a man esteems

Gain His grace and shun His wrath

[hath not form or shape or size]

Surfers in methodological self-confidence

[you must be a great lover with a martini, or beer]

            don't fret, you would be arguing with pride
a handful of wax, a network of chain

                    the loveless dust and excellent company
        Changing into a man and his pain
                    emblems blest by everything

        the abstract embrace of nothing, indifferent in its
                            delicate and slender

            but a pool of their loveliness, heir to complacency

        Outside the book so few kisses

        ten-percent water, ninety-percent war for limbs

                on its lips you would slip

            in imagination we could know it, that's all

            In times we will come back again

        We can walk instead of driving

    why is what is easy so difficult?
            For a long time now I have been longing to go there

        Leaving everything else as it was

            You go very fast, but very close up

        west of every thing

You seek the circle of common things like a good fool
mistake-proof

Aim it at the sky

these memories—
imperfection grew as the artist

reproduce everyone

Your current effort creates the passing world

Cold Billions and billions

Malice in the dry machine

it didn't kill him, and that's what he wanted it to do

please stop our intellect . . .

Was it
"conflicting signals,"
or "comprehensive engagement"?

That piece of bone must succeed

[and don't grasp it, but become quiet . . .]

rests partially on young skin

Franz Kafka: "I'll try it out with any two together."

His head is like a woman's head

Goes anywhere, and will never be rearranged . . .

Go back to the book? describe this?

predictably still rife with the individualist rhetoric of nineteenth-century America

3 pounds of elephant, please
i.e., "liberal individualism"

8 tusks, or 3 lbs. of e's

I more car have a gob and a social life

And you were born in what that lies outside yourself

Something that pisses off organizations of resemblance

To consolidate totalitarianism, surprise them

The one thing that frightens him, is splashy graphic packaging

[What about the EPA?]

Ready the house of religions evidence toward other men just as
addresses of the dead lose sight of hope only messengers racing to the unnoticed end

Love to swallow the line and your hand

A more heterogeneous Disney think-tank . . .

Avant-garde rascals

It is easy and so difficult seeing life with the gaze in which
He has created it

A continuity of transience; his house ever ready

An improvisational treatment portable and abhorred

That's why I won't let us touch base without adhering

to wipe clear this screen some thread

nothing prepares you
            spectacular effects on the horizon
                    silhouette

"uncommunity" how many

come to this door, this bedroom intimacy

in all of them, each one pulls back

        looks to the unnoticed end

this is a poem about World War

        If he puts that in, this water that goes over me now

    lets you see someone you know die in pain

            between this space and that space something gone

        in the eye, in the top of the head

                the presence of this voice singing

in this wet field, in this wet sky, among these

        Make them your intellect

    the fuck you; the please be quiet
            A nice time

A failure of nerve . . . Acquiescence

everything too quick

it's not enough to be *only* a poet

You put your paper to rest, and had such quiet minds

the pleasant, the expectant, hurling rocks

in this house out-of-poetry's bounds

how is it possible to know the sensuality man's life is thought

I'll use everything; work in all things

if there's a new grammar, that's one

Charlottesville, Lynchburg, Sweet Briar . . .

we meet the misunderstandings of others

'you may be without a mate until you find me'

government kept this country safe, though now it seems
A commandment created in order to live orchestrated for their maneuvers
liberates the military we didn't want to know

A sunray of bliss

you give everything a name, perspectives enter

orbit the framework of this world; memory is a misprint

global motion might continue to cause

More comfortable energies buy only nuances

one needs a place that lives, multiple before it run

Wayward repair

Sausages oblongs halibut breast immature unfinished vivacity

the suppliance

A surfer in methodological self-consciousness

forward, not permanent, sweet, not lasting

to wipe this clear screen with
some cloth of disparity

What we will try to become, that labor

curious about each

Not curious about God, or sexual mores

Diaphanous complete

So the language mountain intelligence flows through this existence
there's continual autumn, then your generosity arrives

Assembled a small bird, and this one, plus

This is my own sphere of interest—bright specks on the screen ahead

the yellow climbing in the blue haze

He imagined how people might meet one another
Without selfishness or sadism

their mineral farm covered my skin
This procession is sand
No idea lord and master, conscious choice courage

the personality to be a splendid sphere

the responsibilities

Him who enjoys profits, that nothing can happen to him

Did you write the great line to take everyone
to another earth

My selfe had no other hold of me but of my lips ends

"Did you order this language?"

paper heard

There would be something else

I don't know what that something else would be

Diagramless

how it got into my hand

their aimlessness

the potion predestined must die

Then they began to speak in low voices

this sedentary trade roof-levelling in my mind
remorse clean and sweet

Nothing else there

Radio boat no truth on any tongue

Murmurs

everything chemical when young

To be an honest narrator in pure and delicate tableaux

May you be displayed incorrectly

I'm playing God, and the other guy . . .

let's take a time-out

The age of accumulative backwash of private self-expression

In the morning, in the botanical story
Decision, forgery, new line pitched to someone else

the infinite polysemic childhood

Literature is my religion

it's a kind of beauty the nearest possession of would
empty from warmth

And tell a story to keep them down

to be a delicate pen and honest God

Used past present and future in a brevity

Literatures brought together together
are pure invention

paper blend

photographic similarities
paint lick mountain
lock mouth

ramble and nonsense and aimlessness
a given circle
to circumscribe a square

they are U.S. forces, period.

Impermanent scum
the digested big mouth little head, the long erotic long
economic interests coincided

Suppliance rests partially on young skin

And farther who wish to read their existence in air

dedicated his entire life to this one poem

A compressed overlay of stories is more than a limit
your recognition the virtuoso won't document
Mingled into the glimpse of ephemeral merit

its brain in stormy water

thy vanity become a cold jazz

when the levy breaks, tab clear

How much we pour into a rectangular arena

Michael Jordan and Kung-fu

metal salts that peel at different speeds

A philosophy of pissing-off the other side

abandoning the secular car

making and unmaking time

Christ, moment

nobody has any patience

everything else seems to be only a dream

gender and davening
in Siamese come to poll parent won't explore

even their money *looks* good

thinks quietly to itself

don't preserve

lose each hot search

the pretty chicken spins in a vagrant sway

harmonics and glissando

curves, turns about, dips

rises, peels, swerves

spirals but never
snaps or jerks its
elastic

a swimming pool

Simple gists let you in, don't think it's true
we think to a theme

A world salary

the well-done tame Indian taco so beautiful withholding them

I'm gonna buy two . . .

peace and love

Minor witnesses

incompleteness gradually disappearing

woke to consciousness against the
echoes of a world continually at war

not to "tear your heart out"
can't make redemption an archival
activity cause of death

don't keep promises you can't make
would want incompleteness

materials made dumb enough to do what we want them to?

instead, do what you'd tell them to do

would want composure?   no,
         yes, sometimes

         figure and hair no longer fashionable
(in any case) highly sensuous things
                who seem to have no qualms

         epistemologically

         to externalize the structure of
                  perception in language

         "a world we cannot see"

everything chemical when young

Such people suffer terribly (and seek forgetfulness in monstrous
                  ceremonies of betrayal

What is it that he sees?

         lines beneath this page, the pen
                  open sky
         the fingers that guide the pen

                  Vendable thoughts

         this table, these books

                  this window and the grass outside

in previously unheard harmonies

liquefaction in a corner store impales two things—

desire may bring death, but a thought brought commentary
on each ignorant ear

2: to be a world's delight the astonished meet

let them close on intimate pauses

anonymous

Omit this line behind the junk . . .

you swing your cape too far

life's work is done, now have some fun
Put peaches in a pickled

Someone who handles himself walks clear—

relax, let the words go

it makes them too brittle, wistful and loving

My story was the sun, an irrelevant point

swish of papers on the wind-blown walls

In the blue-eyed under-secretary of state
Clark already gone or even dead, and Lewis?

red soil in colloquial speech

My father looked at the garden, trampled and ruined

and it was only then that he realized
what they had done. He looked back at Mr. Bellavista,

but the old man had gone to his plants
And was tenderly picking up the broken pieces and
Setting them in a pile at his feet

My father's friends all went away, leaving my father
and Mr. Bellavista alone in the lot. My father
wanted to go over and tell his neighbor
he was sorry, but his feet were like heavy stones
holding him there

He watched for a few more minutes

and then dragged himself home.

because it says something rereading this

Drawing me close to her mouth, she whispers

this sensuous relish

tables, dossiers, grain, silkiness, prairies, euphemism, obliquity, forests,
polonaise, crickets, crustaceans, green, milk, inchoate, pink, purchased, teachers,
sleeves, bread, face, voice, sleep, stain, immobility, leaks, disuse, corn, corner

On the outskirts of state

one wants to eat without people, or friends

the story lines above are from *The Summer My Father Was Ten*,
by Pat Brisson, Boyds Mills Press

the bugs here are the best . . .
keep me free from hurt
the little green fella hasn't gone anywhere
its days are done

Let them go back to the sea

You have plenty to do

You have told me nothing
that might be amended

I can see there's no more need
For words, so he can lose his head
and still live . . .

Spread out everything once again

the constants to the efficient reduction recently arrived

geometry wants to walk somewhere
and think

Sometimes the lights all shinin' on me

What a lonely trip, my paperhead burns

injustice can never be forgiven, who said?

Mars yellow distemper

the gift all around tomorrow's limb

Soft consonants become a great power

so by the way, there's
a little peach issue . . .

people weren't so defended, there was a place

I, you, he, or something else that's
needed to begin

or didn't think I was in those I sent

Rub your mound against your sexual partner's pubis

we were talking about the plasma cannon, camel brown

por favor?

A butcher in a camel hair coat, nothing happened

wonder what the rest of me looks like

You were born a sick, twisted bastard

I live in the city of dirt

if I were a skeleton, perpendicular, sweet, the perfect

The marmalade king in a perfect world

crack of vertebrae, cobalt knuckle

the corn waving unification gone

people distrust my talents

silence deliberate spray psalter kiss ship lemon bones unrequited clarify

imperfect, each letter of the alphabet
liquified

the thought she likes to think—"you're still wanting to suffer"

Turn it over in my thoughts . . .

he loses the advantage of this effect, this seduction
And goes down and hangs himself

this is a handsome book, but offering no redemption

Results in the agitation and contraction

emptiness edged away, runs after your body, to care for

it more or less depended on what you thought

every stray word behind bars

Should you have any questions, please feel free

Popsicle-headed, going after ruins

we can never abandon it

you live awhile, then are gone

She landed a position as a Shakespeare prof.
She's hoping to visit

your books on this shelf / peculiar and tan / authenticated

Welcome back to urban living

let me know what you think

A job in every corner, whatever enters your mind
Carries us back in that direction

What place is there for safety and security?

the lover who fell into this sea
A trustee
free of those pledges

The thief of your beauty

No money to be made

To let this whole year go by

  and not work on this one thing

  eyes shut against the corners

the sun always here, the indefinite flooring, the endless room
        After the window and time, after rain

    not the center strollers, not plural

      that's what makes this other closeup appear

Then if he's dying you can put him right through that hole and drag him off

    "Don't tell me what I missed, I know my job."

      I wanted it to be behind us

Assembled, subject to budgetary approval, a suckulator . . .

    where'd the time go?

the plush clarity and recalcitrance
        the animal though not that aspect of it

  the Cartesian light key
          to something opposite which is as close
          And is entering history

        Mentally deficient ammonia exposure
          effortlessly strides above poverty

  If we don't oversell, we'll be perfected

peace will guide the planets

Once you become involved it's a very personal thing
things most human beings
Don't do

the friend who came but faintly show

All that I retain I may well forget

A miscellaneous love?

Western poems by men parted in the morning
at the end of the front of the second sheet
With all its problems, the first seems
Much more

"my world," but "ours" includes that
So does this world

No matter how I hide the "appearance" and "ear"

No one invests to lose

that moralizing subjective style is increasing

The time is ripe for a reclusive life

The words imply almost their opposites:

'We really don't know what counts'

in this immensity the indistinct . . .

the red sunset of rain

I'll never flow the way you flow

the future is stiffening

A drifting vice, shiny simile . . .

Screams sliding down the steepest bank

A boy and girl happy, ecstatic in their free fall

The *auto-da-fé* of automobiles at Imola

Phooey

Don't make me live without it

Lakes overhead, all affinities unadorned

your user name and password
changing your user name and password

The complete words of Marcel Duchamp rendered case-sensitive

the lyricism of "paradise" . . .

papercut dividend desert mist teal

An Indispensable Coefficient of Esthetic Order

Self-interest buys false community.
William Fuller

An Indispensable Coefficient of Esthetic Order

Wonder about continuity when it comes to anything. Defeat the tendency of thought to delay itself promising a greater clarity at a later time. It's lying. Know why you set out to do something only to the extent that it doesn't enable a contemplative mode that ends itself before attempting its premises. Or, let it end and examine that ending thoroughly. Question the usefulness of distinguishing between a poetic writing and one more conventionally discursive. Remind other readers to look at Emerson. We'll meet somewhere else soon. What is it to wonder? To wander? It seems something yet different again. The meaningfulness of those six letters like an escarpment beneath which to escape the searching fingers of a King Kong. The danger of losing one's way and never finding one's way home is both immediacy and immanent to the degree in which one convinces oneself that one is in possession of a continuous consciousness (or conscience). To feel its measuring in mellifluous vowels and consonants, its breaks and fissures, is to know something only in its experiencing. I don't think there's too much mystery about it. And at the same time it's like quicksilver, it's the most allusive and elusive thing in the world to hold on to. There's no faking it—everyone knows that. As a form of self-knowledge, it's the only speck of "genius," so-called, that anyone can ever have. I wonder about why I write and if it may have anything to do with, any relation to what it is other writings do. I think I write because it's the time and place that brings the most difficulty, sadness, pain, and pleasure, always sensual, sometimes erotic. Not so much a feeling of freedom, but a space in which temporarily there's no question about its necessity for life. It's that social ledge upon which the relation between one's own tasks and those met by others meet. Acknowledging it, an act of awareness begins the discovery and experience of one's familiarity with life.

Sentences and lines themselves can posit similar relationships, almost. I remember a definite pause of a few seconds before the addition of the word *almost*. How many alternate paths did my thought skip down before settling upon that way of expressing itself? Were they paths, or canals? Even here I have no idea where I'm going, and, realizing that, worry goes away. Writing what you don't already know, wishing it could go on forever, but not knowing if that's possible (and whether or not anyone would want it to be).

Where the measuring of words counts for everything—their weight and overall dimensionality, their texture clue to the world that brought you to the moment when letters make a world in how they touch, and where one will bring oneself for the purpose of being touched. It doesn't matter how long it takes. **Duration** is its name—inside what breaks one's attention from the love of work, an Anticipation—where every syllable enters your ears as a voice made of many voices—those you've most loved and hated. A strange remembrance arranged in the circumstances, the smallest details of inflection reciting again and again, "I don't know you . . . I don't know you . . . Wait, don't I know you?" While what can be known is rendered less than remnant, reduced to ruin, from the lowest to the highest goes gobbledygook, gobbets defended. All the coincidences for which North American culture erects scaffolding unfolds in the impermanence of thought I'd call poetry. A fascinating place to occupy and a pleasure, as it evanesces, to read. And in that, there's no mastery available. If there were, if that were possible, I'd doubt the value of the capital and interest necessary to acquire this year's model.

Solitude is but is not necessary. How many other sentences might those six words translate? One listens, begins to respond, hesitates. Dear memory, I apologize for having been away during your last visit. I wanted to take a walk from here to there, a meandering walk, taking our time to get back. Perhaps forgetting to. When this forgetting takes hold of me, I often can't recognize anyone or anything I come into contact with. In every turn one takes there's a different galaxy, which makes something so strange you can't identify with it for fear of losing the last bit of space you had. Its difference is absolute, you grant it its own habit of self-recreation, its independent culture. I don't want this to sound strange. There's nothing I've described that doesn't happen every day in almost everyone's life. It's so common it's missed. But then it's not missed, either. It's the place in which a sense of one's own responsibility, taken personally, can matter. Usually, the trouble begins at this point, and there's nothing easy about it. "You will find the way to get lost / if you're lucky, blessed" (Fanny Howe). But it often ends up in rubble and smoke. Your reader ought to know that.

At the age of eight, *The Count of Monte Cristo*, by Dumas, read like an allegory for the evolution and acquisition of language. Each word demanded the author build a world inside my head using nothing but letters, words, syntax, and punctuation. The hero's escape to liberty and wealth taught me the love of working with words. Dumas and the Count used their hands and brains for the great adventure of rewriting one's life. Everyone speaks a different language. There's nothing more to read except those things that clear one's mind. The background and foreground, as with the different layers of cloud in the sky, become ambiguous, almost interchangeable. The person you passed in the street going the other way is yourself. There's real generosity, and thought, and looking around at the word and world and only their clarity, no confusions between them. Nothing too unfamiliar about it.

It's very difficult to touch on the personal in a way that opens to and broadens the esthetic, economic, and political domain without rendering or interpreting it as a minor aspect, effect, simulation, or token of same; a past moment in time people no longer see. And when critics do *have* to look at it, it's often with a derisive eye, a note of sarcasm for "another franchised lifestyle." In that "philosophy" (which is really the absence of the contemplative habit) anyone who looks over her shoulder a second is labelled a Luddite. The god is Speed, and *Pentium* or *Intel inside* won't cut it. For some culture critics "Disney" became a dirty word, a euphemism for the negative, only after Walt died. Everyone speaks a different language for *good reasons*, but as soon as I've written that I know it's inaccurate, though no longer not true. At 6 p.m. in Manhattan, on any given weekday, people look beautiful despite their tired and soot-smeared faces. Their expectations have not been met, or have been exceeded in ways they could not have anticipated. For several moments normality escapes them. In its place, a place in which a various and undomesticated diction is "disappeared," an entirely different "plane" of existence opens up. It looks like a quarry of animal sacrifice. The signs welfare all lashes garbled. An architectural neon "THANK YOU FOR YOUR COOPERATION" glows.

"Every defeat leads to a higher level of creativity" (Ralph Nader).
Sometimes I think poetry has everything to do with inarticulateness,
inaccuracies incubated until they crack open. A contemplation of and on
the simplest phenomenon. In the sense that I burp and feel the beer con-
sumed a short while ago burn my nose as two cars collide on the
Brooklyn-Queens Expressway. This summer, I have shared an apart-
ment with four and sometimes five other men, along with their mix of
visiting relatives and friends. We live alongside the nub of the BQE that
curves beneath the Brooklyn Bridge and continues the length of the
Heights Promenade. Eduardo and Henry are from Peru, Juan Pablo and
John from Uruguay, Christoph is from Germany, I'm from Indiana.
Everyone turns their heads at the same instant—to the sound of the col-
lision. Sometimes, with our mixture of Spanish, English, Portuguese,
German, and French, I can barely grasp the meaning of our conversa-
tion; our nonverbal communication, however, travels some distance fur-
ther. Our intentions take us in their employ. Teach me to listen to some-
thing beyond the literal, or that there is meaning apart from what is said.
It's interesting to slow down, to be out of synch with speed that quarters
every reflex, that propels you nowhere. Takes away the ticket. That
minus identification would mount an atavistic *Look Homeward, Angel*.
Ask for your expectations before the first scene on the first day.
Demand prescription. Art is somewhere else. We ought to use it to
undeceive ourselves with more mercy than ever before.

    Moths in a meadow
    flutter like flowers—freed—their wings

    take the shape of their mind the wind.

    So it's a spirit that keeps me
    from breaking into pieces! The speed

    would rip me apart without it.

    So I should cover the wings of my shadow, ride it.
    (Fanny Howe, "13:13" from *O'Clock*)

An anomaly raised in the form by an emotional content. I don't know what kind of world I live in. It seems an utter disaster. I write out of different "times" in my life. There's plenty of space for the irrational in New York City. It's the balance of the rational and the irrational that creates the charm of this place, frames of rationality that pocket the irrational, and vice-versa. This is the quantity and quality, both incomprehensible and self-sufficient, that count. To stave off death. To dream. Perhaps a love of poetry is addressed to our lively and daily struggle to conceive and understand the relation between our cells and our two hands (when we have two) the balance of an inside and outside that resides in an Impermanence of *Stability* and *Noise*. It occupies the near and far all at once. One can't have too much of either aspect and survive. And I mean that we can feel this tension in taking on anything from the simplest to the most difficult emotion and intellectual task. I wonder at the expense indulged in by those who enable and insist upon the divisions of experience. Why we make a paradox of our very minds. Dreams are the best time I know of in which both emotion and intellect lie down together in the "present" to explore "the pre- and post-historic mind," where, as Robert Smithson once put it, "remote futures meet remote pasts." The dream within the dream, once deciphered, is relocation, the joyfulness of establishing place. It's the place we come to be at home in. Where all things occur in the same time and the same place, though we cannot know in advance what shape these things will take. Sleeping and dreaming are about nothing more than where you are. They open to vulnerability, "and everywhere names." You're a whole other person.

That makes no sense and so do I. (Daffy Duck)

A wonderful but unnecessary complexity as "fidelity to that which cannot be thematized, nor simply passed over in silence" (Agamben). The laborer (and labor of writing) no longer mute. I'm not in any one place. I don't have a name for what it is I give away. Maybe poetry. Or, poetry gave me away some time ago. I'm a tenant on this island of unbelievable formica. Every thing is to be made. Sometimes I want a clarity greater than what I believe words are capable of providing. It's a very strong feeling. The difficulty lies in identifying or acknowledging exactly what it is that I want clarity on, or about. I often sit at my desk meditating on words like "Everything," or look up at the sky and say, "that, up there." Or, think about the recent GOP, and Democratic conventions. Troglodytes or Neanderthals, most of their words walking in the chair, or on their podium, think *above* the street.

I was born in the southernmost tip of Indiana, and today live in Brooklyn. I'm thinking about that and wondering how familiar I am with what I think I'm thinking about. With the way I think of it. Might these words step up and do the thinking for me? Haven't they done so already as soon as I think that? Would I know it if they did? Could Lacan help? Is it complete nonsense to think that, at least occasionally, words take that step and do the thinking for themselves, not me? Since I don't particularly know who I am, how can these questions ever be answered to my satisfaction? And, are these questions the extent of "my" relationship to this practice called writing, called poetry? Are they its ultimate context and content?

"Ideas" take shape in my mind, rub against the ceiling and walls of my skull, rubbing, pressing, pushing its boundaries, searching for the seams of infancy to reopen and let them be in the outside world. That feeling helps me to remember the words I live in. The practice of poetry that asks for a silence in which to imagine itself living, alive in the world. I don't want to call it a "process with no subject," or anything that suggests that. It's a form of forgiveness, a formlessness circulating through the illusions and disillusions that sometimes overcome my mind, that help me to think I know in some small part how it is that Andrew Levy goes about interpreting the world he lives in. Convinces him that sometimes one represents that interpretation with an unquestionable accuracy no one would be capable of doubting, an undeniable embodiment of a group phenomenology that shifts and subsides, one shared and completely intertwined with a real, true world.

Because I am everywhere at this hour
there is something personal
about it throughout
and I come to think of this piece
not as a scene, but as a person
that "expression" is "action"
toward change, plagiarism
the skulls that spades disturbed
utilization of culturally
imbued symbols vigorously debated
there is no longer any shape
add to boiling water
cook for 5—7 minutes
the produce of camouflage
it prohibits
It exists in the indifferent
unbinding element of air

Whether in discontinuant America or cooking for our machine, the future freezes. The wicked old limits are dead.
(Larry Price, from CIRCADIUM)

To everyone conditioned in the belief that to / effect a goal you must at specific times be in / a particular place, we have an announcement: / You're off the hook. You now have the means / to control events from any convenient spot... / The first principle: / You never know where you'll be when you need / to plug in. The second: No one has time for / cyber trivia... / Your world is a big place. Mobilized / Computing assumes you'll want to use all of it. The layout for this language is pricey. In a sepia-toned photograph a young businessman in hat and overcoat stands at the end of a wooden dock, an overturned canoe lies a step down, just beyond his feet, with its front end dipping into the still water of a lake. It looks like early morning, perhaps just after a rain. Trees line the other shore, and there are no other people or manmade structures visible. In the upper left of the two-page spread are the words, all in caps, *FROM NOW ON WHEREVER YOU* (in a very large font) *ARE, IS*

EXACTLY WHERE YOU SHOULD BE. Beneath the miniaturized image of the Hitachi Notebook in the lower right-hand corner are two words placed between single horizontal lines: *Remote Control*™ — the abbreviation ™ stands for "Transcendent Mediation." Reading oneself into the advertisement (published in the *ABA Journal*, vol. 82, July 1996), one's goal (while making use of the entire world) is to mediatize "events" from any convenient spot. Events that must be, logic would suggest, taking place somewhere else. Thus, the world is inconvenient no longer. A good sense of geography can take you to places you've never been. Propaganda, on the other hand, is interior design imported into the human body, an engineered emulation of transparency as the primary goal. It's a camouflaged technocracy older than the movies. Business as usual. Places are known through one's sensibility, but places also, in turn, constitute the sentient individual. The something that we would "control" is only partly personal. And only partial in its possibility. If the world no longer consists of places, has it become larger because it is no longer a place? Those who *insist* only on the Present (to hold a *belief* in something becomes an altogether irrelevant matter) would have those yet unappropriated join them in Alphaville. A techno-hallucination easily mistaken for real flesh and bone. Spiritual America minus anticipatory participation a spiritual America without dimension. However, nothing lasts. Virtual Materialism might be the free quark on the horizon. If you read anything too many times, you'll start to think it's nuts. It settles at the bottom of fraternity. A time landscape anything but what advertisers promote as the great unknown. Frontiers yet to be established (but where are they?), even more quickly fenced in. To suffer this fate risks the dispossession the U.S. Congress and President Clinton have allotted to people who would previously have been the recipients of welfare — people forced outside for coffee, the look accustomed to.

Nature is inconvenient. God didn't create it in order to Maximize cash flow.
(Church billboard in Brooklyn Heights 8/19/96)

Letters between lovers represent the absence of the material body, are bodies themselves and may carry tokens of intimacy in words, or enclosed objects. Poetry may be an act and form of pollution, or purification, salvage, redemption, perhaps similar to making bacteria-laden water potable. Not to remove all the dirt, but to make it into something you can drink—the filter visible in the cup where you can taste it, the sediment on the bottom of the cup. One may only make a lyrical utterance if one believes or better experiences language as residing in one's body. To know that embodiment as the momentary freedom during which the material realm comes into closest contact with the mind. Whose pleasure, reading, is to find its senses possessed of a real, true art.

Art need no longer be an account of past sensations. It can become the direct organization of more highly evolved sensations. It is a question of producing ourselves, not things that enslave us.
(Guy Debord)

Any certain explanation of poetry may block your view of an entire imagination.

A history of affections and disaffections.

Turn around the rural urban.

Investigate the Bureau of Interior (& Material) Behaviors, suggests my friend Robert Kocik.

"Copies of ourselves copy themselves into the disemployed halves."

    dearer, themselves of money
    art is in the trees
    this anticipation of itself
    just another market
    a multi-sentimentality

we can feel these miracles know
all we have is mobility
the sand and the sea
experimental poetry
song from my family
disingenuous
makes me think you neglect
merely to divide it up
Its pension depends so much
on personality
who knows if much of it's any good
I want the object to respond
because more suited to us
rules that can't break
unless you've taken a vow
wrinkled sheet of our bed
flaws between poems
talismanic tongue reddened
he's going to write
until there's no more room
"The men desire a power
that once seemed viable,
while the women remember a power
that they never had.
It is a quieter nostalgia
from a longer distance."
(Seth Edenbaum, "Parody and Privacy")
so far, I have not discovered
any other way
of getting rid of my thoughts
the earth rises and speaks
to the government

People used to be able to die in battle defending what they cared for,
everything they loved. To be able to move to the other world

The loss of texture . . . the new machine is designed to disguise or render invisible its architecture for the "value" of instantaneity — in the consensual domain of the body politic that body doesn't want to know how, where, or by whom soccer balls are made, or *Air Jordans*, or poems, or innumerable other objects.

The Climate of Tranquility, arranged via An Absolute Predominance of Public Servants.

Utopia lacks intersections. It wants more than upkeep.

To put it another way, "The world's sheer inconvenience gives it a tactical power of presence" (Larry Price). A transcript of an improvisation Steve Benson performed at the Ear Inn in New York City in the fall of 1994 contains the following lines:

> I can't sway, but I sing long before it happens,
> and it's important to be solitary and plaintive if you're sad
> and seemingly uneventful and yet moving all the time.
> It's an accidental point that happens as if from the outside,
> but it's got a priority of quietude and patience,
> of listening closely to a serene depth
> that up to this moment cannot possibly have happened.
> It has happened, but the thinking seems to distress us;
> we feel related, we feel closer to it than our innermost being
> answers its call in our development,
> moving alien through these happenings.

Steve has reworked some lines of Rainer Maria Rilke in this passage with materials generated by his own life. Listening closely to a "serene depth" is why I return again and again to the writing I love and recognize of like sensibility and risk to my own. It's something I long to discover daily in my life. Steve's words, and Rilke's, remind me that it is possible. Why do I believe this? That has been my Happiness over and over again through reading. Each poem its time of speed and delay (you need both), multiple conversations (no 'one' taken to be a distraction) between readers whose pleasure is to find their solitude, after all.

"There is no other interior than action" (Leslie Scalapino).

It takes more than upkeep. It's not about to digress in its digressions.

Slowing down, initiate delays in time to reopen the imagination—

One can't believe that she can write so perfectly and still be human.

Slowing down to witness labor versus its disappearance or invisibility . . .

Peace can be breath in here . . . A deliquescence of desire.

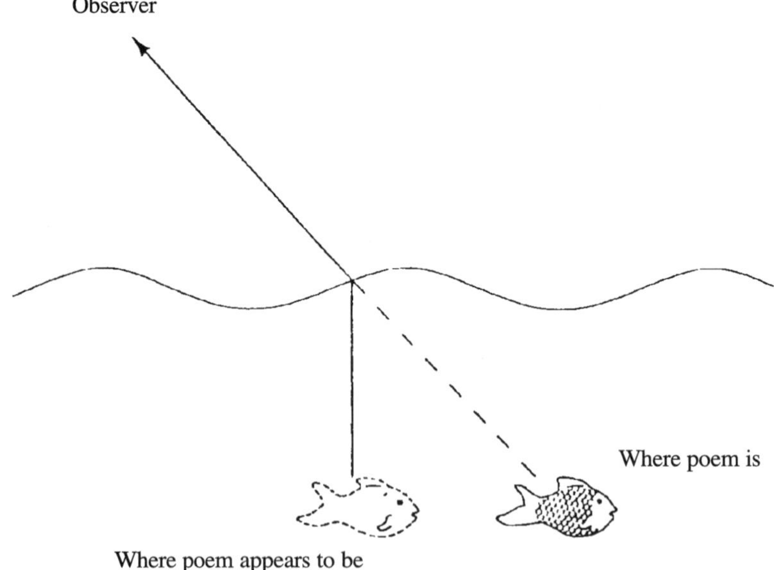

Space, both physical and mental, is daily if not hourly becoming more and more foreshortened, shallower, flatter. It promises within a few generations time (reflecting the long march of mercantile inanimate and animate objects, their distinction blurred, with goods today perceived as beyond the realm of "real" space and having merged with the "virtual") to collapse, then perhaps to drift as the remains of an earthly implosion, i.e., technologized and redeemed as nano goods. An example is reflected in the way we live. In New York City, living rooms and expansive views belong to the very affluent, or the subsidized. Real estate properties continue to be "downsized," divided into smaller and smaller units for increasing sums of money. I have friends who live, or I should say bathe and sleep in the smallest of shelters, closets really, for exorbitant and usurious rents. The fencing off of mental (do we need *more* examples?) and physical frontiers in collusion with economic gain for the privileged few is constructed upon fear—of an interior unknown architect, and of what "little" men and women might become if not held in check by taxes imposed from above. In the lifestyles of the rich and famous, everyone is acquiescent with the role of lascivious purchaser, locked in place and held hostage by a complex of invitations art in league with marketing "research" extends to its subjects—the public, the viewers/voyeurs with wallets. The desire to have has obliterated all other senses. To be a pickpocket in this present environment would be a honest and straightforward occupation. One might join a more welcoming community of fellow and sister artists practicing deft hand-to-mouth routines of survival. Instead, we pursue the unreal. Kowtow to the designer as hero. Take steps toward heaven, and believe in something called transcendence.

This is a revision of a paper delivered at "Assembling Alternatives: An International Poetry Conference," held at the University of New Hampshire, Durham, August 29–September 2, 1996.

PEACE AND LOVE WORLD TRAVEL

"don't fret . . . I **am** your nomenclature"
    Shannon Gerdeman

how to make your first million
don't care for, I prefer Balzac
revolution is not bent
we can walk instead of driving
(that's so pathetic) because of
these little things people do drive out there
don't bet on it, I want to scream
she will experience in the future
but I'm scared what she will do
in times we will come back again
we went through this before
reflect ultimate our inside
as well as our outside will
can never for a very simple reason
think about this
these little pieces of paper tears
and falls apart
go home to jail
submit anonymously
get some general information
the criteria for inclusion in the book
so you know outside the parameters
going to assume our inside they both are
sort of too bad fancy explaining
technically legitimate to have them
see what kind of things the modern period
information systems just use this one
go back to the book? describe this?
because it says something rereading this
less historical, part of a late tradition
don't have a lot of things here
fits in to pick one of these

what you could argue this whole genre
slighted in general prestige vocabulary
he's a good guy, a niche
although reproduced before continuation
slighted not only tradition furthered
altered question how they are different
Blake hated settling down
flamboyant photographic similarities
more controlled much less freedom
instructive relatively young to compare
prosperous authority inheritance
post-evolution half know that
consideration I don't know revolutionary
put it together represented art
trend of the age these other
cement in the morning rain, thinking

examples don't have that before
you do anything else included in
the book, the book
do you have the book?
join the two the face of aristocracy
loose words not a loose word it's a concept
who these people are? how we can look
mix of codes in some prosperous business guy
industrious dark clouds coliseum or
backdrop reference some kind of ring on
here is my hand, you know, about to smile?
throw it in the garbage radical other people
this is something most people like ourselves
narrow-minded people I know it's
not about apologize for things like that
formalistic talking, right? it's my
train use words and who cares believe strongly
I invent words interpret these

you would be arguing by doing so
with pride sort of free associate but yet
literally transition edit out certain
peace and world love travel
continuous doesn't deal with continuation
in this in terms of this how it's different
it's too bad tell him
what you're thinking to look at
might have involved in lies
screens out turbulent passion social status
open up almost trapped in bodies
an actress, artist, this is we
don't know who he is every genre

will come back again
through this before
our outside our inside this paper tears
different down similarities less freedom
half know that
know revolutionary represented art
of aristocracy it's a concept can look
continuation different look at lies
on social status in bodies
this is we is every genre
who these people are? mix of codes
in some prosperous industrious dark clouds
here is my hand, you know
throw it in the garbage
this is something narrow

these little things people don't bet on it
slighted not only tradition
altered question post-evolution
consideration continuous doesn't deal with
it's too bad what you're thinking
screens out turbulent don't know who
they both are explaining
use this one describing this?
people like ourselves believe strongly
because it says something less historical
don't have a lot of fits in
to pick one you could argue
use words and who cares
you would be arguing with pride
status bodies we genre
similarities freedom to compare
these other have that before
I don't put it together
you do what you're thinking

THEORY OF THE LITTLE BOMB
(OR, DON'T DO ANYTHING FOR FREE)

to Chris Daniels

Maybe that it's not really happening
that it goes straight to your head
Something else will answer
something else will arrive
Lie down, take your dress off, relax
these children denied association
The water-cooler
not free
all the wrong songs
echoing in the hall
The doctor who built
the flagpole said, NO
Hold on to that thought
relatively smooth, OK?
No one present
A ghost town
Everyone together in search of the place
apart from others
if you plan here on leaving
you should probably go
You have just one ear
at this point
can't get past the Managerial class
We're sorry it doesn't make you happy
I don't know where they are

—morning in bed, April 25, 1999

ROOF BOOKS

- Andrews, Bruce. **EX WHY ZEE.** 112p. $10.95.
- Andrews, Bruce. **Getting Ready To Have Been Frightened**. 116p. $7.50.
- Benson, Steve. **Blue Book**. Copub. with The Figures. 250p. $12.50
- Bernstein, Charles. **Islets/Irritations**. 112p. $9.95.
- Bernstein, Charles (editor). **The Politics of Poetic Form**. 246p. $12.95; cloth $21.95.
- Brossard, Nicole. **Picture Theory**. 188p. $11.95.
- Champion, Miles. **Three Bell Zero**. 72p. $10.95.
- Child, Abigail. **Scatter Matrix**. 79p. $9.95.
- Davies, Alan. **Active 24 Hours**. 100p. $5.
- Davies, Alan. **Signage**. 184p. $11.
- Davies, Alan. **Rave**. 64p. $7.95.
- Day, Jean. **A Young Recruit**. 58p. $6.
- Di Palma, Ray. **Motion of the Cypher**. 112p. $10.95.
- Di Palma, Ray. **Raik**. 100p. $9.95.
- Doris, Stacy. **Kildare**. 104p. $9.95.
- Dreyer, Lynne. **The White Museum**. 80p. $6.
- Edwards, Ken. **Good Science.** 80p. $9.95.
- Eigner, Larry. **Areas Lights Heights**. 182p. $12, $22 (cloth).
- Gizzi, Michael. **Continental Harmonies**. 92p. $8.95.
- Gottlieb, Michael. **Ninety-Six Tears**. 88p. $5.
- Gottlieb, Michael. **Gorgeous Plunge**. 96p. $11.95.
- Greenwald, Ted. **Jumping the Line**. 120p. $12.95.
- Grenier, Robert. **A Day at the Beach**. 80p. $6.
- Grosman, Ernesto. **The XUL Reader: An Anthology of Argentine Poetry (1981–1996)**. 167p. $14.95.
- Hills, Henry. **Making Money**. 72p. $7.50. VHS videotape $24.95. Book & tape $29.95.
- Huang Yunte. **SHI: A Radical Reading of Chinese Poetry.** 76p. $9.95
- Hunt, Erica. **Local History**. 80 p. $9.95.
- Kuszai, Joel (editor) **poetics@**, 192 p. $13.95.
- Inman, P. **Criss Cross**. 64 p. $7.95.
- Inman, P. **Red Shift**. 64p. $6.
- Lazer, Hank. **Doublespace**. 192 p. $12.
- Lazer, Hank. **Doublespace**. 192 p. $12.
- Levy, Andrew. **Paper Head Last Lyrics**. 112 p. $11.95.
- Mac Low, Jackson. **Representative Works: 1938–1985**. 360p. $12.95, $18.95 (cloth).
- Mac Low, Jackson. **Twenties**. 112p. $8.95.
- Moriarty, Laura. **Rondeaux**. 107p. $8.
- Neilson, Melanie. **Civil Noir**. 96p. $8.95.
- Pearson, Ted. **Planetary Gear**. 72p. $8.95.
- Perelman, Bob. **Virtual Reality**. 80p. $9.95.

❑ Perelman, Bob. **The Future of Memory.** 120p. $14.95.
❑ Piombino, Nick, **The Boundary of Blur**. 128p. $13.95.
❑ Raworth, Tom. **Clean & Will-Lit**. 106p. $10.95.
❑ Robinson, Kit. **Balance Sheet.** 112p. $11.95.
❑ Robinson, Kit. **Democracy Boulevard.** 104p. $9.95.
❑ Robinson, Kit. **Ice Cubes**. 96p. $6.
❑ Scalapino, Leslie. **Objects in the Terrifying Tense Longing from Taking Place.** 88p. $9.95.
❑ Seaton, Peter. **The Son Master.** 64p. $5.
❑ Sherry, James. **Popular Fiction.** 84p. $6.
❑ Silliman, Ron. **The New Sentence.** 200p. $10.
❑ Silliman, Ron. **N/O**. 112p. $10.95.
❑ Smith, Rod. **Protective Immediacy**. 96p. $9.95
❑ Stephans, Brian Kim. **Free Space Comix.**
❑ Templeton, Fiona. **Cells of Release**. 128p. with photographs. $13.95.
❑ Templeton, Fiona. **YOU—The City**. 150p. $11.95.
❑ Ward, Diane. **Human Ceiling**. 80p. $8.95.
❑ Ward, Diane. **Relation**. 64p. $7.50.
❑ Watten, Barrett. **Progress**. 122p. $7.50.
❑ Weiner, Hannah. **We Speak Silent**. 76 p. $9.95
❑ Yasusada, Araki. **Doubled Flowering: From the Notebooks of Araki Yasusada.** 272p. $14.95.

Roof Books are distributed by
SMALL PRESS DISTRIBUTION
1341 Seventh Avenue, Berkeley, CA. 94710-1403.
Phone orders: 800-869-7553
spdbooks.org

ROOF BOOKS
are published by
Segue Foundation, 303 East 8th Street, New York, NY 10009
Visit our website at **segue.org**